CHARTIST SONGS,

AND

OTHER PIECES.

No. 1.

By William Hick,

SECRETARY OF THE LEEDS TOTAL ABSTINENCE
CHARTER ASSOCIATION.

LEEDS:
PRINTED BY J. HOBSON, MARKET STREET.

1840.

CHARTIST SONGS, &c.

ON THE WHIG REFORM BILL.

No greater swindle ever rose,
  To mock the erring soul of man,
Than the Reform Bill we'd expose,
  Since the great world its course began.

They told us we should have our *right* ;
  They swore the millions should be free ;
That this first *offspring* of our might,
  Should lead us on to Liberty.

But when we took the reptiles in,
  Who swore then love alike to all ;
They basely sought our aid to win ;
  To sink us deeper still in thrall.

How patiently we look'd for bread,
  Which promise on the breeze was borne ;
Our confidence to this had led ;
  But O, alas ! they gave a stone.

4

They soon denied the truths they spoke ;
 And vilely centring all in self,
O'er solemn pledges oft did joke ;
 Their boasted virtue bowed to pelf.

Thus was the ruling passion seen :
 Their darling *order* claim'd its power ;
And we, neglected, all have been,
 Poor trembling sheep while wolves devour.

They've made us worse, they've made us poor,
 Then built us bastiles where to dwell ;
Heap'd infamy from door to door,
 And would have sunk our souls in hell.

What tears of blood preserved on high!
 What groans from many a victim slain !
But wrath shall blast their author's cry ;
 Their prayer to heaven shall be in vain.

Who love or pity e'er denies,
 When claimed in plenty or distress ;
No pity wins from out the skies,
 No heavenly love shall ever bless.

They've sent us " rurals" o'er the land,
 And spread their net with fiendish care ;
Where the torn flags of freedom stand,
 They seek the last lone shred to tear.

5

With iron hand, and iron sway,
  They rule us with audacious pride ;
And when we would the wrong gainsay,
  Their prison gates are open'd wide.

The people's friends in dungeons pine ;
  And some are banish'd " far away,"
Whose only fault, whose only crime,
  Was that, to break despotic sway.

Alas ! we weep, we sigh for these !
  We do not, cannot seek, in vain !
They shall have liberty and ease,
  And see their country once again.

But here, must yet remain unsung,
  One-half the bloody deeds they own,
Whose curse is on the people's tongue,
  And heaven's all-dire avenging frown.

For soon shall cease this upas race,
  To blast the nation, and devour ;
Their deeds shall only leave a trace
  To say who once had rule and power.

But ah ! one lesson has been taught,
  Which ne'er shall fade from memory's dome ;
To trust alone in *native thought*,
  For deeds of honour yet to come.

We'll do our *thinking*, and confide
　　To none for freedom's happy call ;
Ourselves the suffrage will decide,
　　And give the heavenly right to all.

THE PATRIOT'S RELEASE.

———

Tune,—" How fine has the day been, how
　　bright was the sun."—Watts.

How joyful the morn of the Patriot's release,
As he springs from his cell to meet friendship
　　and peace ;
Where he knows all his torture and thraldon
　　shall cease,
　　To begin his blest warfare again.

With a strength not his own, and a love all-
　　divine,
He battles once more for his own native clime;
And the laurels he earns with a glory shall
　　shine,
　　That must ever reflecting remain.

Through tumult and anger he urges his way,
Where the peoples' sad wail breaks the still-
　　ness of day ;

7

And he asks the real cause of their want and
    decay,
   While the land affords plenty for all.

Then he bids them unite, and he points them
    the road,
Where the rights, all their own, are by freedom
    restored ;
When in millions they rise round the hero
    adored,
   And liberty comes at their call.

THE LOVERS IN FREEDOM AND SLAVERY.

FREEDOM.

They sought the bower in days of yore,
When the heart was stricken at every pore,
And loves romance—they read it o'er :
        The lovers in freedom.

The soul was full, yet sought increase
In the love that chains, or gives release ;
Each pillow'd a head on a heaven of peace :
        The lovers in freedom.

The whispers that hung on the evening air,
And that softly fell on the ears of the fair,
Was the way that they play'd at echo there :
        The lovers in freedom.

8

O'er the noise of mirth, and the jarring tongue,
The mantle of woodland stillness they flung ;
And nothing but wildwood notes were sung :
              —The lovers in freedom.

The present was all in all to them ;
The future was only a brighter gem;
No tyrant might their peace condemn,
              The lovers in freedom.

But time in her change, by rapid pace,
Hath carried away this happy race ;
The lovers of old we cannot trace,
              The lovers in freedom.

SLAVERY.

By the weary mill, in the darksome night,
The stunted girl, in her unwash'd plight,
Meets her pale-cheek'd boy by the lamp's du'
    light ;
              The lovers in slavery.

Not with eye illum'd at the parting rays,
Of the sun at the end of his glorious blaze ;
But the listless, o'erwrought, sleepy gaze,
              —The lovers in slavery.

Where, where is the look of purity,
The modest glance and the laughing e'e,
The child of the patriarch's family ?
              The lovers in slavery.

At the entry end, where the rabble meet,
Or the stroll a'down the smoky street,
Is the spot where the modern lovers greet :
       The lovers in slavery.

Or dark in the path of guilt and sin,
Which gulphs at last its victims in ;
An end, the lords of mammon begin:
       —The lovers in slavery.

Away, away, to hell or death,
To the soul of him who gives his breath,
In support of the system's blighted wreath :
       The lovers in slavery.

TO BE SUNG ON THE MORNING OF

FEARGUS O'CONNOR'S RELEASE.

TUNE,—" Then let the trumpet sound, &c."

YE millions now awake, and from the spot
    wherein ye dwell,
This morning up, your Feargus is about to
    leave his cell:
O'er the mountains let's go meet him, with
    banners all of green ;
And the world shall soon confess, how true our
    hearts have ever been.

10

CHORUS.

Yes to meet him we will go, will go,
To meet him we will go ;
With the Charter Flags all in our hands,
We'll make a gallant show.

O, was he not our Charter the first to take in
hand,
And did he not its principles go spread through-
out the land ;
Against all opposition, from foolish friend or foe?
But he never once would turn about, or the
glorious task forego.

Yes, to meet him we will go, &c.

Aye, "onward" was his motto, when oft we
thought him mad,
But we little knew, like him, that then, our
case was half so bad ;
For he saw our sad condition, and he knew the
factions too,
And swore no good could ever come, from the
orange boys or blue.

Yes, to meet him we will go, &c.

And alike he disregarded, the middle "sham-
boys" train ;
He taught us never more to trust to other's
brains again ;

11

But firmly all uniting, *ourselves* to lead the van,
We might with ease the Charter win, for uni-
versal man.

Yes, to meet him we will go, &c.

Through floods and fire he ventured, to strike
the moral blow,
Where sternly stood corruption up, and shew'd
her brazen brow ;
For Freedom and her children, he hurl'd the
thunder on,
And like a warrior in our cause, he saw the
battle won.

Yes, to meet him we will go, &c.

Ar this they took and bound him, determined
he should die :
ough sick, within the felons' cell, they ordered
A he should lie ;
  id there through lonely nights, in fever's rage
and gloom,
He pray'd that death might ease his pain, and
seal his final doom.

Yes, to meet him we will go, &c.

But soon his fare was altered, and health re-
turn'd again,
And now in mind he fights for us, nor will he
war in vain ;

12

The sentence of corruption, expires at last, and
    we
Are hieing on to welcome him, our hero well
    and free.

     Yes, to meet him we will go, &c.

To lead us on to victory, he comes the kind
    and brave.
A chieftain he deserves to be, who hates the
    tyrant knave :
O'Connor is that chieftain, and with millions
    by his side,
Will soon the royal people's cause, by moral
    means decide.

     Yes, to meet him we will go, &c.

FROST, WILLIAMS, AND JONES

———

Tune,—" Mercy's Free."

Hark! hark, the people's voice is loudly sound-
    ing ;
    Frost be free ! must be free !
The solemn news thro' all the land rebounding;
    Williams free ! must be free !

This voice so loud, the throne shall hear,
And echo back, our wishes clear,
Let all the banish'd ones appear !
    Jones be free ! Jones be free.

13

Up, up, the canvass to the gale is spreading,
  On the sea, on the sea ;
 nd fast the steamer sails, no danger dreading,
  O'er the sea, o'er the sea :
 e cliffs are covered by a host,
They wave adieu along the coast,—
Exhult their labours are not lost,
  To set them free,—set them free.

Away, away, she flies across the ocean,
  Bold and free, bold and free ; [tion,
The steersman cheers, and every hand's in mo-
  Blythe and free, blythe and free !
And proudly on, they breast the wave ;
And soon they reach the *convict grave* ;
And to the patriots good and brave,
  Quick they flee, quick they flee.

Again, rejoice ! we come to give you freedom,
  The mandate see, mandate see ;
The millions call you back to come and lead 'em
  Till they're free, till they're free.
Your chain has gone ; you are slaves no more ;
And soon afloat, where the billows roar,
You speed to reach your native shore,
  And be free, and be free.

They come at last, they land, we shout them
  Brave and free, brave and free ; [home,

14

The patriot band have weather'd out the storm,
   Brave and free, brave and free ;
Their sufferings will unite us more ;
And oft we'll talk all their trials o'er ;
And all the land shall ring from shore to sho...
   Of the free, the brave and free.

WHIGGERY'S FALLEN.

TUNE.—" Babylon's fallen to rise no more."

Hark ! the morn of freedom brightens ;
   Up ye workmen at her call ;
Spread the news that so enlightens,
   With its touch, the souls of all :
Victory sits upon your brow,
   And shall ne'er forsake it more ;
Whiggery's fallen, fallen, fallen ;
   Whiggery's fallen to rise no more.

Hill and dale again are blooming,
   Verdure rises o'er the land ;
Britain is once more assuming,
   What she long might well command :
Millions bold are proud to see, her
   Tyrants fall from shore to shore ;
Whiggery's fallen, fallen, fallen,
   Whiggery's fallen to rise no more.

15

Now are burst the chains that bound us,
   Now we hail the jubilee !
Freedom once again hath found us,
   For the patriot soul is free.
Soon they raised the voice of thunder,
   And the palm from tyrants tore ;
Whiggery's fallen, fallen, fallen,
   Whiggery's fallen to rise no more.

T'skilly lords are now defeated;
   Malthus hangs his fiendish head ;
Well they know the men they've cheated,
   Never more will thus be led.
Union on our hearts is written,
   While we sing the triumph o'er,
Whiggery's fallen, fallen, fallen,
   Whiggery's fallen to rise no more.

All the ills that hell could muster,
   All that malice could prepare,
Round their standard firm did cluster,
   —In deceit beyond compare.
Now they are by all detested,
   And this torment pains the more,
Whiggery's fallen, fallen, fallen,
   Whiggery's fallen to rise no more.

Yes, the treacherous gang shall find us
   Past their power to gull again ;

16

Words from them no more shall bind us :
  We will all their wiles disdain.
Places, pensions, all are flying,
  Now their short-liv'd joys are o'er :
Whiggery's fallen, fallen, fallen,
  Whiggery's fallen to rise no more.

Laugh we now at dread oppression,
  Captive is Captivity !
Now shall truth have loud expression,
  By our friends from dungeons free.
Factions all shall own the Charter,
  And our sun shall set no more ;
Whiggery's fallen, fallen, fallen,
  Whiggery's fallen to rise no more.

FEARGUS O'CONNOR.

O where is O'Connor, the bold and the brave?
Entomb'd in yon dungeon, but still not a slave:
No prisons can bind him, his heart is still free,
And bold is his front, as a mortal's may be.

They thought to have slain him, while fill'd
    with disease,
So with felons they placed him, their malice to
    please ;
But no fiend-devis'd diet, nor cold or damp cell,
Could obtain him a passport to heaven or hell.

17

For 'twas heaven ordain'd that his people should
    hear;
When Normanby learnt what such ministers
    fear :
Then backward he slunk from his treacherous
    aim,
And his lickspittle " shallows" were told to
    refrain.

And now all alone in his own furnish'd cell,
He thinks o'er their insults, the malice of hell;
And laughing he labours to pickle a rod,
'That shall smite all his foes, and the foes of
    his God.

Already they've had just one peep in his
    " glass,"
Where, each wore the real head and ears
    of an ass ;
And now are they silent, nor mock, nor deride,
For the laugh has been turn'd to the opposite
    side.

But ere long they will skulk like a fugitive
    band,
And their Ishmaelite race will be banish'd the
    land ;
For as loathsome as toads in a dungeon they've
    grown,
And the seal of their doom is their self-earn'd
    renown.

18

For we saw him, by chance, in his prison one
    day,
And blythe was his heart, and his spirits were
    gay ;
With sternness resolving no atom to yield,
To battle triumphant, or die in the field.

Hurrah for O'Connor, the bold and the brave,
The foeman of traitors, of tyrant and knave ;
The pet of the millions he's fought for so long,
The pride of the poet, the boast of my song.

THE LABOURER'S REGRET.

Mourn Britain o'er thy desert lot,
The cheerless hearth, and lonely cot :
A peasantry so much the pride
In days of yore,—they now deride :
Since wealth and luxury have spread
Their ghostly charms around the head ;
In vain I look, no virtue see,
The land hath lost her truly free.

'Twas once the labourer's envy'd right,
To boast of freedom in his *might* ;
His hand the ready title gave,
And none might dare to call him slave :
But ah, how alter'd is his fate ;
The laws have ta'en his *real* estate ;

19

And now no vestage can we see,
Of all the truly great and free !

Behold he begs from door to door,
The able bodied, strong, but poor ;
Or cast upon the tide of life
With helpless infants and a wife ;
A passive thing before the gale,
Nor hope, nor anchor, in the vale ;
And this, the remnant we may see,
Of all that once was truly free.

Reduc'd, to beg for leave to toil ;
For leave to quit his native soil,—
To gladly list the schemes that say,
We wish to send you far away :
And in some *craft* as old as time,
That sinks him ere he reach the clime ;
Or in its hold, by stench, at sea,
Destroy what once was great and free.

And this, that tyrant hands may hold
The nation's wealth, the nation's gold :
That thieves may rob, as statesmen dress'd ;
For this the people are oppress'd :
The few may only live and reign,
The many may not dare complain ;
Such class distinctions all may see,—
Unlike a nation great and free.

20

But equal rights and equal laws,
Must soon decide the people's cause:
Or soon will fall the threatening blow
That lays the proud usurper low ;
Or bury in the whelming strife,
The injured husband and the wife,
As hand in hand they fight to be,
What once they were—the truly free.

THE CHARTER! THE CHARTER.

Tune.—" Jacob's Ladder."

As Britain lay prostrate, her foes on the throne,
Her statesmen all plotting, each one for his own,
The people deluded, and plundered of all
Beheld, as from heaven, their rescue let fall.

CHORUS.

The charter, the charter, the gift of the brave,
The nation from wreck, & its people shall save ;
Then onward, then onward, our motto shall be,
To ask for the charter, and live with the free.

Through much tribulation, through dungeons
    and strife,
Our patriots have trod, and would forfeit their
    life ;

21

For freedom they battle, for freedom they die,
Or live in the laurels she brings from the sky.

Chorus.—The charter, the charter, &c.

And shall we, less noble, the standard let fall!
And slink from that chieftain who gives us his
    all ?
O ! no ; we have shouted the onset, and we
Through blood, if they choose, yet, the victors
    will be.

Chorus.—The charter, the charter, &c.

From clouds of distress, we shall see the dawn
    break ;
The dawn of a day that the tyrant shall shake;
And down from her throne, shall corruption be
    hurl'd ;
When again Britain rises,—the pride of the
    world.

Chorus.—The charter, the charter, &c.

Away, then, all sorrow that springs from bad
    laws ;
For away all distress must depart with its
    cause :
No hunger shall haunt us where labour we give ;
The workman is worthy,—the workman shall
    live !

Chorus.—The charter, the charter, &c.

22

We ask for no more, and demand we no less !
And who dares refuse us ?—the wrong let him
    press !
The field is before him, no danger we dread !
'Tis better to die, than while living be dead.

    Chorus.—The charter, the charter, &c.

THE BRAVE AND FREE.

Tune.—" The Sea."

The free, the free, the brave and free,
The bold, the gay, the kind is he :
No stain shall mark his open brow !
No ruthless deed his overthrow !
As the air that he breathes, his soul is pure ;
Untaught in her ways, no vice shall lure.
I love the free, the brave and free !
And with him I would ever be !
With an eye of love, and a hand to lend;
He never deserts a needy friend :
But, alike with his purse and his influence, he
Shall merit the title of brave and free.

And when the strife of his country calls,
The spirit of him the foe appals ;

23

With untirring zeal, no danger dreads ;
But onward presses and victory spreads :
The weal of his home is the star of the brave ;
And the land of his birth he will die to save.
I love the free, the brave and free !
And will follow his footsteps whither he be ;
For he never can live in the bonds of a slave,
Nor the tyrant love, who would dig his grave :
But he vows for ever his curse to flee,
And merit the title of brave and free.

And when by Fame his brow is crown'd,
He seeks again that spot of ground
Where first he drew his infant breath ;
With his homely fare, and his rural wreath ;
With the plough and flail, for the battle shield,
And his tended flocks in the open field :
O ! then he's free, the brave and free !
Aye, just as I should wish to be !
With one whose love is a cloudless sky,
And the tender glance from beauty's eye !
Till the trump shall sound of eternity,
He'll merit the title of brave and free

24

A RECITATION.

**THE IMPRISONED CHARTIST'S WIFE AND
DAUGHTER.**

Daughter—Mother, listen, I would ask
　　　You, what has got my father?
　　　He has not been at home so long,
　　　I wish he'd come and hear the song,
　　　He taught me on the Charter.

Mother—Ah, no my dear, the Whigs have ta'en
　　　Your father for that Charter ;
　　　And now he in a dungeon lies,
　　　Where dreary night sweet rest denies;
　　　—On worse than bread and water.

D.　In prison mother ! can it be ?
　　　I thought the Whigs were kinder ?
　　My father's kind to you and me ;
　　And widow Worth has said, that he
　　In bread would always find her.

　　I'm sure old widow Worth will cry:
　　　Now father's gone, she'll hunger !

25

M   And we my child, and shall not we?
Perhaps to suffer more than she,
   If father stays much longer.

D   But Mother, what has father done,
   To vex those Whigs so naughty?
M   Done! my dear; why nothing more
Than cry " be free !" from shore to shore,
   " And down with tyrants haughty."

D   Why mother, did not once those Whigs,
   (For father told me how they shouted,)
And did not they talk in this way,
And swear if once they won the day,
   The tyrants should be routed ?

M   Yes, yes my love, they promised well,
   Till workmen got for them the places ;
But soon as did the traitorous band
Assume the reins to give command,
   They mock'd us to our faces.

They hedg'd themselves all round & round,
   With new made friends in numbers ;

26

The franchise of the ten-pounds men,
Was loss to us, and gain to them:—
   These wink'd at all their blunders.

And on they went, embolden'd thus,
   With power to show their nature ;
The country's weal was not their aim !
But *places*, to supply the claim,
   Or serve some cringing creature.

Commissions, rurals, and bastiles,
   The art of centralizing,
Has only made our taxes more,
Depress'd our trade, and taught us sore,
   The way of pauperizing.

D   But mother, do not tell me this ;
   My father was no wicked traitor !
You know, he taught me evening prayer,
And ere I sought the morning air,
   To praise the great Creator !

My father would not injure any !
   Then why is he in prison ?

27

M Because, my dear, by freedom taught,
The workman's ills he kindly sought,
   By legal means to lessen.

He raised the charter standard high,
   To bring the pining millions round it ;
And there exposed the cruel wrong ;
The fell deceit ; the lying tongue ;
   The system as he found it.

Success was great: they felt the blow ;
   Their craft was now in greatest danger,
And, like themselves,—to lying bred,
"Old women, frighten'd were," they said ;
   "The Queen,—it would derange her."

And "treason" cried, for words of truth ;
   And only aim'd against corruption :
They call'd these meetings modes of riot,
Disturbing peace and general quiet ;
   And national destruction.

And under guise of love of "order,"
   They seiz'd the leaders of the charter ;

28

In hope to stay the rising call,
Of freedom as the right of all :
   And carry on their barter.

But ah, their cruel prisons, Ann !
   Thou must not know what they endure!
Thy tender heart would break to hear,
A loving father's trial there ;
   For *words* and *motives* pure.

A long twelve months he lingers there !
   And God alone can tell us love !
If e'er from out that spot he tread,
The living father, or the dead !
   And where shall we remove ?

Their bastiles must receive us both ;
   And oh, my grief does sorely press !
                [*weeping.*]
They'll part us love, they'll part from me,
And I my child shall seldom see !
   To fondle or caress.

D   Nay mother, nay, you make me cry.
   I'll kiss you now, and make you well ;

29

I'm sure my father will not die !
I'll pray to God who reigns on high :
 He'll bring poor father from his cell.

Come mother, come, "the Book" hath said
 Where father often lov'd to read,
The wicked shall not always 'scape,
Though wily be the course they shape,
 For wrath is on their deed !

I'll be a Chartist, so shall you !
 And when my father comes we'll go !
I'll wave my banner in the breeze,
Till every tyrant's blood shall freeze ;
 Till freedom shall become the law.
Then, though they take us, we will be,
To freedom martyrs, or with freedom free.

THE FACTORY BELL.

Alas, I hear those factory bells !
Which on the air so loudly swells :
Haste happy day,—the day that tells
The banishment of factory bells.

30

From out the bed each cheerless morn,
Are British children early torn ;
And forc'd to toil, unceasing, dread,
To earn their scanty share of bread ;
Through cold and rain they shivering go,
Through hoary frost, and deep-laid snow ;
Nor dare that call the child rebel,—
It is the voice of factory bell.

The voice of mammon cries, away !
To toil ye must ; or else no pay :
The painful truth the widow knows,
And pining, 'neath the stroke, she bows ;
Yet often broods o'er moments fled,—
Her lov'd one, who so lately dead,
Had cheer'd her path, and wip'd her eye,
And borne her sorrows,—hush'd each cry ;
While now, the offspring of that sire,
'Mid wasting death, unheard, expire
By slow degrees : alas, the spell,
On widow'd hearts ! from factory bell !

They come, they go, the weary round :
No other help for them is found,

31

Since tyrants have the power to wield
The laws,—a nation's strongest shield ;
This lust of gold, hath borne away,
The rosy cheek, and reverend grey ;
And youth must wear another hue :
And years ! alas, no years we view !
As now at forty, men expire ;
The young old men—the factory sire !
Haste happy day, the day which tells
The banishment of factory bells !

Hobson, Printer, 5, Market Street, Leeds.

Milton Keynes UK
Ingram Content Group UK Ltd.
UKHW050818260424
441811UK00007B/426